SHADOWMOUTH

Meredith Oakes
SHADOWMOUTH

OBERON BOOKS
LONDON

First published in 2006 by Oberon Books Ltd
521 Caledonian Road, London N7 9RH

A catalogue record for this book is available from the British Library.

ISBN: 9781840026795

Characters

MAN

MOTHER

BOY

PAUL

DAISY

shadowmouth was first performed on 1 June 2006 at the Sheffield Crucible Studio with the following company:

MAN, Tony Guilfoyle

MOTHER, Joanne Howarth

BOY, Ryan O'Donnell

PAUL, Eddie Kay

DAISY, Imogen Knight

Director, Dominic Leclerc

Designer, Liz Cooke

Lighting Designer, Mark Jonathan

Sound Designer, Gareth Fry

shadowmouth

MAN The ward was full of old men

    Babbling, wandering about

    Counting up to ten, not reaching it

    He was fifteen, fresh as a rose, apart from
    the bandage

    His mother was saying

MOTHER I've brought his pyjamas from home

MAN He never wore pyjamas

MOTHER He won't wear them

MAN No

MOTHER He resents me

    I try

    He resents me because I try

    I put on lipstick

    He says I'm putting on an expression

    I make myself presentable

And it feels like a betrayal

Sweetheart!

BOY Mum

MOTHER Look at you

BOY I'm

MOTHER Slippers, where are your slippers

You must have your slippers

BOY Mum

MOTHER They don't sweep under the beds

They actually sweep things under the beds, I've seen them

All sorts of things

Dressings, tubes, fruit, flowers

BOY I'm sorry

MAN I didn't know what to say, any more than she did

She'd made sandwiches

MOTHER It's nobody's fault

Is it

MAN   She put the sandwiches on the bed cover

As if he were going on a train journey,
leaving her small on the platform

I live alone

I'm fine with that

In summer, I make a bed on the balcony

And when the neighbours' music has
throbbed itself to a standstill

And the silence is beginning to be louder
than the traffic

And the city breathes out

That's when I can almost bear to…

I first met him in a cinema

They had a knife

A collector's item, I'm sure

Anyway, they'd collected it

Still, I was honoured they showed it me

It bespeaks a level of trust

Also on my side

He was homeless, he said

Well

I have the space

I don't believe a place of safety is a place
you lock

It's a place you decide not to lock

He was new to my method of tea making

I've discovered after years of experiment,
if you keep the tea in the pot all day you
can simply put this much into a mug and
top it up with hot water, you can hardly
tell the difference

It's an efficient method

BOY   Thanks

(*Sips tea.*) Interesting

MAN   I found his presence extraordinary

His bag his shoes his jacket

His hand around the mug of tea

BOY   It's very kind of you

MAN   Not at all

MOTHER   He let the cat on the good white couch

That I bought after his father left

He deliberately

And then of course it descended into a row about the drugs and

I didn't mean it

Perhaps I did

As revenge

Because I couldn't help him

I told him it was for his own good

I ripped up his posters

MAN   He liked hamburgers, Radiohead, Frida Kahlo

Footballers' Wives

None of his socks matched

He made a hammock for his stuffed owl

MOTHER   His father was an animal

Why did I marry him?

Because he was an animal

End of story

For me, inside

It doesn't show

I wouldn't give him the satisfaction

MAN   He told me, even as a kid he used to sneak out at night

He used to climb out of the window

He didn't want any pane of glass or piece of wood between him and the moon

He was in love with her

He loved her bleak little face shining coldly so far away

He felt a chill that was a thrill looking up at her

He loved her even more at midnight than in the evening when she swung down close

In the evening she loomed large like a mother

But at midnight she rode high in the sky
like the skull of a little princess, and when
he looked up at her, he could feel the
vertigo of immense times and distances,
seen from her vantage point

He didn't want anything as much as he
wanted that cold thrill

At times when he missed her, he'd steal a
few mouthfuls of his mother's scotch, and
then a few more

BOY   School's, you know

Not where I am in my head

MAN   School

School people

Sniggering with embarrassment in the
face of anything true

They know they're faking it but you'll
never get them to admit it, never

And they practise cruelties large and
small on you, if you show them up

BOY   Sports day

Cheering and yelling and acting as if it mattered

If you didn't, teachers noted your attitude problem and kids threw your lunch over the fence

It was the one thing they definitely agreed about, you had to act as if it mattered

Sports day was when I discovered I could be there and go somewhere else in my mind

Really go

I went into a wood with huge leaves

And leopards

MAN   Daylight people scare me

The ignorant certainty they profess

The confident ring of their footsteps

Their desire for everyone to be up and in harness

Day is always fresh and new

Exhausting

Night is what you return to

Where everything that used to be still
lingers

And Juliet still talks to the moon

He used to walk by the rail yards in the
moonlight

BOY   One night, I reached the centre of town

It was like discovering a whole unknown
tribe

People awake at night

Like me

Going about their business in the middle
of the night as if it were the most ordinary
thing in the world

While everyone I knew was asleep in bed

All the rules were turned upside-down

Drink, drugs, visions and sex were
everyone's serious business

While the business buildings, the
government offices, the gallery, the
museum, slept like dark forgotten giants

There were lit up places floating like
boats on the city darkness, and in them

were pirates and ruffians, girls with
smudged eyes and bare flesh, drinkers
staring down into wells of alcohol, fat
hairy men in black leather, women in
bowler hats, people with cigarette holders
and rings on their fingers

It was like seeing through the skin of the
city down into where it had always been
like this, century upon century

It was like seeing the hidden life now
visible and glowing, everyone decked out
as the self of their dreams

I didn't know who I might see lining up
to the bar

Christopher Marlowe

The Queen of Sheba

I'd never seen a floor with so much dirt
on it, the dirt of centuries

Fag-ends in drifts

Grit piling up against the skirting boards

And people slopping drinks as they
passed, calling to each other across the
noise

The air was at saturation point with
alcohol, smoke and sweat

The place felt ready to burst into flame

It was here

Whatever would make me real

I was in the room with the animal

I could see its rolling eye, its velvet
mouth, its foam-flecked shoulder, its huge
flank

I could feel the heavy stumbling of its
hooves in the straw

I loved it

MAN   You see, I couldn't see anything wrong
with

On the contrary

In his love of what he saw and
experienced, he seemed to me to be
magically beautiful

And through him, if I had him near me

I could see the whole world as magically
beautiful

He adorned my life

He probably brought the drugs to school
to hold on to like good magic

As much as to sell them

He was expelled of course

He found himself a job at a filling-station,
casual employment

MAN   What about your age

BOY   Identity card

MAN   What

BOY   It says I'm eighteen

Look

I made it

MAN   Yes

I see

BOY   No-one asks

This is the city

PAUL   How much

BOY   Cocktail shaker twelve twenty

PAUL   It's got a mark

BOY   I can't take money off, you tosser

PAUL   See the mark

It's damaged

BOY   I know it's damaged, you damaged it

PAUL   I've done bar work

The manager had it in for me

I said, life's not worth living, if I can't give my friends a drink

Twat said I couldn't control my temper

So I nutted him

MAN   He met a girl there

She was older

A cradle-snatcher

She took him out, bought him things

Glamorous

DAISY   I want pizza

BOY   But it's

DAISY   Shut up. I want pizza. Where's the fridge

This is what you've got in your fridge

A lemon

A lemon

How do you people exist

Let's go shopping

BOY   It's the middle of the night

DAISY   I'm going shopping

BOY   Sit down before you fall down

Sit down. I'll go shopping

DAISY   Come here. You're not going anywhere

He can go shopping

Hullo!

BOY   Quiet you'll wake him up

DAISY   Hullo!

BOY   Shut up he's asleep

DAISY   He won't mind

Your landlord

Landlord!

BOY   Shut up. No-one's going shopping

DAISY   All right darling

You darling

Are you angry with me darling?

Come here

I love you

God

MAN   I was glad he was straight

No, really

The worst thing is hope

I've always watched boys

Ever since I was a boy

Vaulting over railings

Kicking cigarette packets

Eyeing girls

I was always watching

Learning how to be one

I never did learn

BOY   Morning

MAN   Good morning

BOY   Sorry about the noise last night

We didn't disturb you

MAN   Hardly at all

BOY   You don't mind

MAN   No

BOY   You're not upset with me

MAN   Why would I be upset

BOY   So everything's all right then

MAN   How are you this morning?

BOY   She's nuts

I think I'm in love

MAN   Well, of course he knew I

He was indispensable to my peace of mind

His beauty was my redemption

That room, when he was in it, was satisfied

It was filled

I didn't even have to think about it

That's how absolutely solved the problem
of that room was

Before when it was empty it was on my
mind obscurely

A sense of something lacking, barely
conscious

A worry about lopsided bookshelves or
bad chairs or the room somehow eating
itself

Suddenly everything in the room was
perfect, glowing and secure

And I could get on with making toast or
writing my history of monasteries

Knowing he was there

While he

I don't know

Entertained, why not?

Or smoked

Sharpened pencils

Listened to the music of the spheres

He said he found himself dragging the
knife across his wrist

And suddenly awoke to a knowledge of
what he was doing

And that's when he came and showed me

What had he done

What had he suffered

It was the last thing I ever thought he'd

It was the opposite of everything I
thought he

He was life, generous life

He wasn't even distorted in the minor,
unhappy way most people are

There was nothing twisted, mean, narrow
or obsessive about him

No mark of pressure, no deathly misery

Just a profusion of loveliness, dreams

Yet he

How could I not have seen?

What had I been looking at?

I half expected the shine on the hospital
floor

To throw up earth and boulders

And how could he have had to go
through this alone, when I

Loved him

I shuddered with terror thinking he might
have died

And I'd been happy, useless, criminally
contented

And what was I going to say to his
mother?

The shock would be

MOTHER   Of course, it's not the first time

He did tell you

MAN   No

MOTHER   Are you all right?

MAN   He'd told me nothing

        I felt

        Like an orphan

MOTHER   I want you to know

        It's nothing to do with you

MAN   Like an orphan

        Selfish

        In his darkest hour

        But I did, I felt cheated, bereft,
        insignificant, criticised

        While hating myself for feeling like that

        But is it possible to love someone without
        needing them?

        How would you know it was love, if your
        very existence and comfort didn't hang
        on theirs?

DAISY   I thought he and I were together

        I was

        He wasn't

MAN   I know

DAISY   The little sod

        I've been outsmarted by a fifteen year-old

        It's all secret with him

        Secretive

        I feel like tearing him apart

MAN   I know

        Then she went out and bought him a watch, to cover up the scar

        One isn't consistent

        Perhaps it was really as he said, a thing secret from him as well as from us

        A lake of tears, rising unnoticed, until the banks broke

        And after that

        Emptiness

MOTHER   What happens

        When you come out of hospital

        You might like to come back home

BOY I

MAN He said he wouldn't

His mother didn't try to dissuade him

She wasn't very confident

Especially after that

Whereas I revived

I meant something

I could do something

He'd be saved

I got rid of the bathmat

Bought some new towels

New records

Daisy cooked for his homecoming

DAISY Are you hungry?

Do you want to sleep

What do you want

MAN I'll make some tea

DAISY Do you want tea?

BOY   It's strange

DAISY   What

BOY   Everything

DAISY   Us, are we strange

BOY   Everything

DAISY   Where are you going

BOY   The toilet

DAISY   Do you want us to go with you?

MAN   Strange

Yes, we were

I found I was always wanting the world to put on its best face

The one that would woo him and keep him

The perpetual question was

What face was that?

Should I empty the ashtray (or would that prompt thoughts of mortality)?

Should I not (or would that prompt them even more)?

Should I switch on the light (or would
that be too bleak)?

Should I let the darkness grow (or would
that be too symbolic)?

What did he see?

What lifted him? What threw him down?
What reassured him? What made him
afraid?

What if that which reassured him actually
made him afraid because it seemed to be
trying to reassure him?

I bought fruit to nourish him

A pot of daffodils to cheer and strengthen
him

I'm not claiming any of this was rational

I felt like some sort of kaleidoscope,
with all surfaces splintered, shaken up,
disturbed and disturbing

We drank tea, played chess

Normal as could be

Nothing was normal

I kept imagining how things might look
to him

What might set him off

I began to hate the daffodils

Their sturdy cheerful brutish flowers

I hesitated too long over the chessboard
and started seeing dead horses

I dreaded his mother's visits

MOTHER   I wanted him home but he chose this

Do you know what I've decided?

I'm not the problem

He's the problem

If I think of it any other way, I'll go quite
mad

It's good of you to let him stay

I hope he's grateful

I think he finds me far too boring, don't
you sweetheart

I was bohemian when I was young

Cockroaches in the saucepans, that sort of thing

You're lucky to have kept your cool

Whereas I have an almost irresistible urge to get the hoover out

Perhaps you'll be the saving of him

I hope something will

He's keeping his appointments, isn't he

With the psychiatrist

I'm sure if anyone can make him do what he should, it's you

He pays no attention to me

MAN   She was always trying to make me into her representative

MOTHER   I have absolute faith in you

My friends say I'm crazy

But I know you're a truly good person

A selfless person

If I thought for one minute there was anything wrong about his being here I'd be doing everything in my power to put a stop to it

MAN   I saw each sentence as an arrow
threatening his fragile peace of mind

Or mine

But he

Gave her his washing

   PAUL in.

As for Paul, he was so young, but he
never smiled

He was a graven image

He seldom looked at me

Sometimes a scrap of a glance

Moving his face would have been giving
too much away in the poker game of life

His nerves were always on edge and that
was why he was so still

Once he brought me some opera glasses,
once, a bag full of shoe-trees

Thank you

So many

Are you sure you don't have a use for
them?

It dawned on me

Paul and he were

Oh God

Well of course I kept thinking about times
he'd

I don't know

Helped with the rubbish

Borrowed my aftershave

DAISY   He's not gay

He's just

Too young to know the difference

I'm not jealous

It's him I'm worried about

Laugh at me, go on

Fucking gays

MAN But anyway, I couldn't have invited him
under my roof and just

Above all, in the circumstances

Even forgetting his age

And mine

If he'd wanted

If he'd ever shown the slightest

The fact is, nothing took place

And that was as it should be

PAUL (*To DAISY.*) I'm going now

DAISY Good riddance

BOY (*To DAISY.*) Paul and I are going

Do you want to come?

DAISY Where?

I'll come

MAN My pot plants had drugs hidden in them,
I'm sure of it

PAUL   What are you doing?

MAN   These plants need a good soaking

PAUL   Yeah

MAN   What's the matter?

Jealousy

Not just the fear of loss, but the fear of
being dried away to nothing

A prophetic fear, of course

If a choice had existed between him
being happy with Paul

And him being dead

If that had been the choice

What would I have

Paul made him well

That's the paradox

The three of us went to the shop one
night and stole cloth, for Paul's mother's
curtains

It's never been missed

I'm the only one who knows the stock

The owners are idle and unpleasant

I still work there

The greatest love, they say, is the love
that lets another person be

I didn't want to want anything from him,
nothing at all, just his freedom

That's how I felt, in moments of clarity

You're home early

BOY   I went in the door and Paul was at the
other end of the bar

Talking to the Civil Servant

Bicycle Man

He waved

By the time I got through the crowd I
couldn't see him

I kept looking

Then I waited

Got drunk

Got thrown out

Smashed a window

MAN What do you want to do

With your life

BOY Maybe art school

MAN Art school

It wasn't impossible

He needed the O levels but he could be signed up somewhere, I began making enquiries

He started on a portfolio

BOY Bollocks, it's bollocks

MAN But these are

Not bad

BOY They're bollocks

MAN What's this

BOY I can see it in front of my eyes when I close my eyes

It's a tree with its roots in a rock and the light shines through it and it flies

This isn't anything like

MAN You've only just begun

BOY It will never be anything like

MAN That was the end of the art school idea

PAUL in.

BOY Where were you Saturday

PAUL Where were you

What have you been up to

BOY What have you

PAUL (*To MAN.*) Hullo

(*To BOY.*) What's he looking at

BOY You

MAN He's busy

BOY It's fine

PAUL He's fine

What's your game?

MAN   I beg your pardon

PAUL   What do you want?

MAN   I

PAUL   I know what you want

I know what you want

Nonce

PAUL leaves with BOY.

MAN   I bore it for his sake

DAISY in.

DAISY   Is he here?

Where is he

The little shit

Have you got a drink?

What's that you're writing?

I'm not disturbing you

How could you let him run around with Paul?

Don't you care?

It's irresponsible

It's not good for him, all this

He should be in an institution

He should be locked up

Crazy little shit

And as for you

No, go on with your work

I'll just sit here

MOTHER   Is he here?

The thing is

I'm dead inside

Since his father left

Do you understand what I'm saying?

So when he started having all these
problems I think what I felt, deep down,
was

He was acting out everything that was
wrong with me

I felt so ashamed of myself

I could hardly stand the sight of him

Isn't that terrible

I think he and I have more in common
than you think

I'm a survivor, that's all

Oh God, I don't mean he

But if life's trying to kill you, you fight it

Does that make sense?

Have you ever been married?

BOY in.

Sweetheart

MAN   One could easily spend all of one's time
just living

Steering a course, that's what I felt I

Sometimes they all visited at once

MOTHER   Is he in?

DAISY   Is he in?

PAUL   Is he in?

MAN   I generally retreated to the balcony

PAUL   (*To MOTHER.*) Do you want a cigarette

DAISY   She doesn't smoke

MOTHER   I'll have one

       I've brought your washing

PAUL   Lucky boy

BOY   Yes, aren't I

MOTHER   What do you do, Paul?

PAUL   Oh

DAISY   What doesn't he do?

MOTHER   Are you two together?

MAN   I constantly felt like someone trying to guide a sleep-walker

       Talking sensibly, doing everything sensibly

       My mind in a panic constantly seeing him fall

PAUL   Catch

BOY   What is it

Thanks

PAUL   How much will you give me

BOY   For this?

PAUL   Twenty

BOY   Keep it

PAUL   Don't you want it? It's a present

Give me fifteen

BOY   I thought you said it was a present

PAUL   I got that for you

BOY   Where are you going?

Stay

PAUL   Get off

BOY   Stay

PAUL   I'm going now

BOY   Tramp

PAUL   (*Hits him.*) Don't you ever

BOY   You're just a little tramp

PAUL   (*Hits him repeatedly.*) Don't you ever call
me that again

What did I say

(*Hits him.*) I said what did I say

MAN   I went for him

MAN winds up on the floor, badly beaten.

Of course, he took Paul back again

PAUL   He said he loves me

It's patronising

He wants me to stop him thinking

So he won't top himself

Wanker

He thinks he can get emotional

If he thinks I'd cry over him

Fuck him

BOY   I don't know what's the matter with me

I'll always be alone

Have you always been alone?

BOY kisses MAN.

MAN   I have

BOY   Sorry, I'm sorry

MAN   Forget it

It didn't happen

BOY   I'm sorry

MAN   He called Daisy then

He made her coffee with honey

On his sixteenth, his mother took us out

The restaurant was Italian

It smelt of vegetables being kept warm

MOTHER   What's everyone having?

What's Paul having

PAUL   Nothing thanks

MOTHER   Nothing

PAUL No thanks

MOTHER Is there nothing here you like?

Minestrone?

Cannelloni?

There's chips

BOY Don't you like this place?

PAUL It's OK

MOTHER Does Paul not like this place?

BOY He's OK

MOTHER Are you all right, sweetheart?

BOY Yeah

MOTHER They'll bring us a tiramisu at the end, with a sparkler

MAN It's a cake

Do you like cake, Paul?

DAISY You can have some of my spaghetti

MOTHER And mine

PAUL whispers to BOY.

BOY He'd like some bread

MOTHER   Of course

Waiter!

MAN   I took him walking out of town near the
reservoir

Sitting on the ground with grass waving
all around us in the sun, lit to vanishing
point, substantial and insubstantial, with
the glittering water beyond

I hoped he found it as beautiful as I did

I was looking at the scene, hoping it
would be enough for him

When I found myself not hoping but
questioning whether it was indeed
enough for him

And to my alarm as I tried to hold to the
vision

It started to seem faded

Or like a thin painted scarf drawn over a
void

And I seemed to be seeing it with the
light gone out of it, fading to ashes

As I thought oh no, oh no

Because if it wasn't enough for him, he
might die

And suddenly it wasn't enough for me,
because I'd questioned it

And I couldn't even tell any more why
I'd ever thought it was enough

He was eating an apple quite happily

And I certainly couldn't ask him if he saw
what I saw, in case he did

BOY   I'm glad we came here

I feel all right with you

At home, I can't explain it

The loneliness, looking at the sofa, linen
texture, round fat feet

It's so plump

Sitting on its fat feet alone in the universe,
all dressed up and nowhere to go

And the haircord on the floor

So empty and busy, with a square of
sunlight on it

MAN   Just then

We could have –

The moment was so –

It was so –

It was too –

To use it for anything would have been vandalism

He would have said no in any case

I hope he would

Because otherwise, that could have been the moment that changed everything

One ordinary evening he got ready to go out

In a cloud of Paco Rabanne (mine)

They found his body two days later

I didn't see it, but I keep seeing it

You can be right next to someone and
still they

I still don't know what he suffered

I'm still trying to, I follow all the
pathways, sitting here at night

It's a strange thing

I never saw him weep

And he never said hullo or goodbye, he
was always just there or gone again

Of course it could have been his
childhood, his love-life, something
coherent

Any or all of the difficulties

But if a difficult life made people kill
themselves

Millions would do it every day

Depression, that's a thing people talk
about

In affluent societies

Maybe at the top of the tree, you
see more, you see all the way to the
boundary

And everything between

All this shackled complicated half-life

I stand accused by his death of finding
the world good enough

I don't find it good enough but I can't
find the place

The extreme place where

So many times I've tried to follow him
there

To be company for him

Not leave him going through it alone

But

His wound isn't mine

Perhaps I'm unworthy

I'm left here wishing the world into some
kind of state where he could thrive

The funeral was

His mother had him cremated

Empty grey room, rows of empty seating

Piped music

She cut me

Didn't even look at me

Wherever he was, he wasn't there

His presence was always radiant

You can bring forth all sorts of reasons
why it might have happened

Maybe even read the circumstances in
such a way that it was bound to have
happened

But that's not how it seemed, not at all

I don't understand any of it, not even the
first thing, that one moment he was there,
warm and breathing, the next, vanished

I look for him all the time

In drinking places, or under the street
trees at night

I look for him

Waking or sleeping

In some way, I always knew it would
happen

But not because of any particular
circumstances I could see

It wasn't the circumstances that made me
know he'd do it

It was him, something about him

Nothing tragic, just something

Unearthly beautiful, that you know you're
not good enough for

He climbed into the park to do it

Had a drink

He died leaning up against a big park tree
mottled in the lamplight

Ranks of worshipping flowers erect in the
night air

The small moon visible through the
leaves

A tryst, that's what I really believe

He died going towards beauty as I

Go towards him

He died going towards the life he was
born to know

End.

www.ingramcontent.com/pod-product-compliance
Ingram Content Group UK Ltd.
Pitfield, Milton Keynes, MK11 3LW, UK
UKHW020730280225
455688UK00012B/579